for ruth and my family. also for john cooper clarke, john peel and tony wilson.

thanks to sustaining friends and to those who, for whatever reason, have taken
a shine to some of the stuff i have done and supported me/us. thanks of course
to those people with whom i have made albums and added to the noise – phil
hayes, bruce magill and damian ashcroft.

may the road rise...

the albums:
'Cheap Shots', by superqueens, SkinnyDog Records, 2004
'Royal Shit', by superqueens, Supermarket Records, 2006
'Small Times', by The Orch., SkinnyDog Records, 2010
are out there somewhere, just hanging around

all poems/lyrics, whatever you call them, in
'easy rhymes a.k.a cheap shots, royal shit, small times' are by michael conroy,
collection first published 2012 (c)

book design and various photographs by kayne li lui sang

search the web for more...

Easy Rhymes a.k.a. Cheap Shots,
Royal Shit, Small Times
Michael Conroy

www.fast-print.net/store.php

Easy Rhymes a.k.a. Cheap Shots, Royal Shit, Small Times
Copyright © Michael Conroy 2012

ISBN 978-178035-515-3

First published 2013 by
FASTPRINT PUBLISHING
Peterborough, England.

Printed by Printondemand-Worldwide

Cheap shots:
"cut!"
security and peace
the silent pool star's lass won't say hello
business is business
serving suggestion
state hotel
a bum deal at the arse-end of art
let's not call in the heavy bombers
ladies and gentlemen, doctors and nurses
gotham/metropolis
i'm in the no-show biz

Royal shit:
per ardua ad strangeways
spinning leaf
rat poison
molecular
not for all the e's in england
no picnic
mister, you're a lapdancer
the ghost of billy whizz

Small times:
without trace
living in sin
ingland strip
kenny and the snake
ritual abuse
slaves make my baby's shoes
spectacular times
little rockets

Cheap shots

"Cut!"

my sister's husband's daughter's man
is on four kinds of drip
– you could say he's well connected
for the first time in his life.
the remote control's the only thing
that's firmly in his grip
and gangrene's got the doctors
sharpening the knife.
we're in marlboro country,
on the flipside of the billboard,
shovelling the horseshit
and the hidden costs.
his stetson is a crew-cut and a vacant stare,
his six-gun changes channels
– it's a lightning-tipped repeater.
a lassoo of pure catarrh
stops conversation in its tracks
and he rides the satellite sierras
on a beige and black three-seater.
"howdya feel, danny boy?"
– *"well, not too fucking clever"*
"you giving up the cigs, then?"
– *"i'm too young to say never"*
"i see you're hooked up to a screen"
– *"yeah, it's like a porn film, without the sex"*
"guess you'll have to quit the ballet"
– *"nah, i'll just teach myself some new steps"*
and in the western tradition
he grins at his own jokes
and faces down the man in black
who smiles as he smokes
and he spits a bit of script
at the invisible director
"fuck it. take the battery out of that smoke detector,

i'm lighting up".
and the anaesthetic
fights to keep his thick mouth shut
and the doctors
and my sister's husband's daughter's man
shout *"cut!"*.

Security and peace

i want to be held for forty eight hours
tenderly, by the police.
no questions asked, no lies told,
just security and peace.
i want to be arrested
by their heartbreaking honesty
and tell them *'it's okay to cry,*
my cell is your cell, brother,
we all fuck up badly sometimes'.
i want to read my rights
in the eyes of the guys
and the girls as they all slip
out of the uniform of their illusions,
away from the way of the whip.
i want to help them with their enquiries,
as long as their questions are right,
like *'how'd i end up a gang-member?'*
and *'why do i feel at home in the night?'*
look at the good cop/bad cop's brain,
fried in booze and isolation.
i want to help him throw away the keys
and demolish his police station.
i want to be held for forty eight hours
and smuggle in the means of release,
safe in the strong arms of ex-offenders
who have woken from their dream of police.
and when they hand in their weapons
and turn their backs on their crimes
and stand in the sun on the streets
and say that they're going to start over again,
they'll have security and peace.

The silent pool-star's lass won't say 'hello'

the silent pool-star's lass won't say *'hello'*,
she hangs back, hugs the walls and watches,
knowing not to interrupt his flow.
it might be the end of the frame before
she knows if she's on the mind
that's fixing down the cue and on the score.
it's cold outside and half an hour from home
and dad wouldn't drop her off
and her quiet gamesman's always
switching off his phone.
half an hour in an awkward leather jacket –
that some señor in palma sold her older sister –
half way across the town like a scented packet,
just to stand and watch
and wonder if he's missed her.
half an hour in too much cheap gold –
she hid it on the bus,
but now she strokes it, thinking,
wanting him to notice
she's worn it specially for him,
but he only seems to see trick shots
and only wants to hear the eight-ball sinking.
only the landlord and the other fellas see
and analyse the teenage skin, the legs, the lips,
and as she suffers the saliva glances she
is patient, but obviously pained, and tries
to stretch her jacket down below her hips.
if looks could ever hurry up a pair of hands,
or eyelashes encourage some minor sign,
the surly player would forget his artful plans
and raise his gaze as she whispers
"half a lager, with a bit of lime".
but across the holy cloth

he spreads his knuckles, some in sacred rings,
carefully assessing how to tense his wrists
and, without a smile, tugs on her easy strings
and takes his time and teases her,
using the cue-ball something like a fist.
at last, the pocket swallows up the black,
she grins and leaves the shadows
where she has been ensconced,
but, without speaking,
he sends her shrinking back,
and fills the triangle again,
and settles down to play two games at once.

Business is business

x communicates with y
and z takes ten percent,
it seems you're always
paying strangers rent,
is pimp culture heaven sent,
or can you send it back?
between the penthouse
and the shack
the dealer's wheels
keep rolling back
and forward
like an old zoo cat,
supplying the demand
and demanding the supply
of bads and goods
to suit the stimulated cravings
of the neighbourhoods
who might not
but maybe should
watch the traffic for a while.
the limo driver's
got a baseball bat
to help him
establish that
business is business
and that
is
that.

Serving suggestion

here is one of many
recipes for disaster:
suspend some pale guy
above your little whirling head
and proclaim him god
although you know
he's only alabaster.
serve the green meat
of the mass
upon the stale bread
of cold stone floors
and flaking plaster.
add a little incense
and slowly grill the flesh
over a sea of candles.
fresh roses should be strewn
upon the floor
to welcome guests
in jackboots
or in holy sandals.
bon appetit!

State hotel

this is the hotel de la necrophile,
where money and the right skin
can make it easier.
you can take it lying down or take it doggystyle
– the management will always try to please you.
you might well call this joint *'the living end'*,
as death squads tidy up, take out the trash,
in their unmarked cars to the wasteland
where fires turn dirty thinking into ash.
"cash prizes!"
cash prizes shine like steel traps,
gamblers fingers fill the bowls like cigarettes,
in the cocktail lounge
which rings with dull handclaps,
as the cabaret reveals its non-exotic pets.
maybe the singers come and go
but the songs stay the same,
maybe hookers die
but it's a case of 'vive la game'.
i'm not saying i am no liar
but i've got a question mark tattoo
that constantly desires
to know why i'm living in a first world state
in a third world state of mind.
the satellite of love beams brightly,
pouring out the hardcore: religion and repeats.
heavy entertainers own the networks,
light entertainment
keeps the people off the streets.
hearts break and some of them bleed
on placebo shows selling sensitive creeds,
because the network knows what the hotel needs
– bread and games and holy beads.
it's a circus in here and a jungle out there.

the mc cracks the whip and combs his hair,
he's a democrat and debonair,
he charms lions with the lingo of the liar
while tv crews feed snuff movies
to the greedy wire.
i'm not saying i am no liar
but i've got a question mark tattoo
that constantly desires
to know why i'm living in a first world state
in a third world state of mind.
it's a circus in here and a jungle out there,
and the big cats keep you inside.
the paying guest becomes the passenger
and gets taken for a slow ride.
and outside clouds touch
and the lightning's a bracelet,
it ain't much,
and it gets missed by the graceless.
it's late summer and the cops are faceless
sharks cruising for a taste of a thought crime,
they roll down the windows
and they breathe out the bad times,
like a nerve-gas, all along the breadline,
like guard dogs, howling in the goldmine.
i'm not saying i am no liar
but i've got a question mark tattoo
that constantly desires
to know why i'm living in a first world state
in a third world state of mind.

A bum deal at the arse-end of art

does the camera steal the soul?
do teenage boys steal cars?
is the catwalk sponsored by gestapo?
do models frame the sky like skinny prison bars?
their smiles leak a bitter gas,
they wash their hair in bottled tears,
they say they're sick of being followed
but they're the stalkers in the shadows of our fears.
beatified by zombies
they soar on vampires' wings,
public enemy, private hell,
jerks jerk their strings.
the usual suspects skulk
behind the fragrance and the skirt,
investors and their dobermen
growling in the dirt.
it's a bum deal at the arse-end of art,
nobody cares what's in her,
tough shit for the also-rans
and track marks for the winners.
they can't keep up with the twelve-year-olds,
they can't keep down their dinners.
public enemy, private hell,
sinned against and sinner.

Let's not call in the heavy bombers

there is a gulf between us
and it's not producing oil.
it widens with the sunrise
yet it never really boils
because we have cooled
like old fire mountains.
there is a gulf between us,
you could say it's warm and deep
but sometimes fighters strafe the shore,
just to say that we must keep
our growing distance.
there is a gulf between us
that shimmers with a slick,
which drags down hopeful seabirds
and makes their feathers stick
so they sadly bend their necks, like alcoholics.
there is a gulf between us,
our old land links are gone,
different time-zones cut the map
where a shared noon-sun once shone
but let's not call in the heavy bombers
– beneath the gulf
there is an ancient homeland
which should not be taken from us.

Ladies and gentlemen, doctors and nurses

this place is a casualty department,
all our mouths moan *"nurse!*
give me the x-ray of your attention,
prescribe the lifting of my curse".
it's any gathering of adults,
it's a nightclub, it's a street.
dolce and gabana is the rich kids' bandage,
the poor ones just overeat.
the walking wounded and the basket cases
limp from scene to scene,
hunting out some loving surgeon
with a double life-support machine
(but they'll settle for a butcher
and an aspirin - they'll get by).
bones fuse and nerves dull,
you can even fix a smile.
she says *"we love each other really,*
we just walk a crooked mile".
one man's meat is another's meat substitute
yet no-one can stand alone -
this catch 22 makes mincemeat
of all the turkeys waiting by the phone.
the foot-soldiers and the sacrificial lambs
get dolled up and they drift
into the arms of the venus de milo,
hoping for a fireman's lift
but they just get judo - or fuck all.
and yet
doctors and nurses, plainclothes, exist,
their soft blows heal the breaks,
their tongues apply wild lotions
licking deep into the aches.
these are the good spin-doctors,
when the planet grinds

they help it glide.
untrained, unpaid and unannounced
they appear at your side.
crushed fruit can make champagne,
roses blossom through manure,
natural medicine floods our veins, venom
is venom's cure.

Gotham/metropolis

it's so much like gotham/metropolis this place
that it's a shame we weren't born into a magazine race
with anaesthetic paint shot through our veins,
like a private sea of 'h' to put a leash upon the pain.
the city spreads beneath the wired artist's sky,
with toxic neon jewels poking at your mind's eye
while a love affair with petrol floats high
above the bodies of its lovers and the music of the drive-by.
lead perfume lies heavy on the legs
of the ladies who supply the good-guys with their sex
while angels cook their dinners chewing downers to protect
themselves against their partners and the city's side-effects.
it's so much like waking up inside a loser's trip,
ripped-off role-play routines fill the bubbles of our script.
the stained-glass window's just a video showing 'tales from the crypt'
to a population hooked on being whipped.
crusader points the finger and the cameras zoom in
upon the small time crook and the enemy within
who won't pay protection to the badge of tin
and commits real life - the original sin.
real skin dealing with real phoney times
crying in the shadows at all of the wrong crimes,
while the city boss pukes out the nickles and dimes
and his gang manifesto and other nursery rhymes.
we're so much like children, us folks
we spend our cash on comic truths and never get the joker's jokes.
frightened of the dark at closedown,
scared of our own flesh at bed time,
citizens say prayers to superheroes
but just get vampires hiding from the sunshine.

I'm in the no-show biz

i'm in the no-show business
i am a superstar
i play my lover's body
like sid vicious plays guitar
– pretty vacantly
i'm in the no-show biz
i am a superstar
wherever i am is
not where she thinks we are
and I know she wants to see and hear
the beating of the wings of wild geese
i just act like a machine
and say *"release the grease"*
i'm in the no-show business
i spoil the cheese in traps
i say nowt in any language
i don't mind the gap
'distance' is my perfume
'goodbye' is my tattoo

25

Royal shit

Per ardua ad strangeways

joey's just robbed two grand in cash,
he's still buzzing from the rave in town last night.
he's the ideal son for a fence
or social scientist,
he remembers birthdays and he hates to fight
– that's joey.
and there's love in his life, it's called anne-marie,
she's the mother of all his good trips.
and she's the driver of his mental getaway car,
she dances well, weaves magic round her hips
– that's anne-marie.
per ardua ad strangeways,
through work to our reward,
we've got good reasons for everything we do
but we do not praise the lord.
stanley knife's a stranger to joey
and there's not much hate in his cartoon heart,
he just loves to shop when the shops are shut
and to move like a prince in the dark.
he's never had to spell *'dionysus'*
but good times trip off his tongue,
his home is a block with an i.d. crisis
where the cops never dally too long.
per ardua ad strangeways
through work to our reward...
there's a skeleton stuck in the lift shaft
of some kid who was once joey's friend,
and tonight there's a mood for some witchcraft
and he goes to him and says *"how shall i spend
these two thousand chances?"*
and the bones say *"rave, do dances,
ramraid, make love, crown your girl's elegances
because it's an ugly town and the dark advances"*.

per ardua ad strangeways
through work to our reward...
the night burns lovely, slow and long,
anne-marie and joey's pleasure voodoo makes them strong,
– but they're fighting something stronger.
morning breaks and cash dissolves,
there's a roadblock
and last night's crime is solved.
and what was that crime –
taking tips from governments?
per ardua ad strangeways
through work to our reward..
joey's just got two years inside,
he's still thinking about a lesson that he learned
from when he was a kid
and his friend was still alive,
"there are those who are the masters of fire
and those who just get burned".
but he's glad he spent
those two thousand chances
and he loves the bones that said
"rave, do dances...",
and it is an ugly town
and the dark always advances,
but he'll be a prince of it
and crown his girl's elegances
– when he gets out.
per ardua ad strangeways
through work to our reward
we've got good reasons for everything we do
but we do not praise the lord.

Spinning leaf

who the hell cares about jfk?
'was it the cia/was it the kkk?'
gangsters always get blown away,
it's a rule of their game.
another president bites the dust,
another secret rifle rusts,
one more gambler moaning *'bust!'*
and one less big mouth to feed.
i've been thinking about the egyptians
and their slaves,
how the pharaoh's tomb
meant their mass grave,
and i've been thinking about england,
and us.
'those who pay the most homage
are the most oppressed'
played in my head as we undressed
and i saw the moon out of my window
on egyptian street.
some people need to talk about the shroud of christ,
others get off on poltergeists,
but my mystery, my ufo,
is why you let me see you in the glow
of the moon near my big window
looking out on egyptian street.
ain't got no strong belief,
no god and no relief,
i'm like a spinning leaf,
between the sky and the land.
i'm missing all the bars that could
have made this town good
and i'm sniffing up the smoke
of the amazon wood,
reading r.i.p.'s for things that died

before i got a chance to taste them.
our clever nature wastes them.
some girl i once knew
made the silver thread i threw
into a ring she pulls me through,
years later.
when i think of her i see stars,
i feel like early man,
i nearly hate her.
ain't got no strong belief,
no god and no relief,
i'm like a spinning leaf,
between the sky and the land.

Rat poison

other people,
they are the refuge and the hell.
powerful enough to rub you out
with one cheap trick
yet also strong enough
to bring you gifts
of brightly coloured shells.
they can plant kisses
on your hot, tired face,
spray you with their metabolic perfume
or stun you with their home made *'mace'*
of mundane or treacherous design
and so unleash
the spirit of the rat race.
illy finds it easier to let go
of all his dogs of hate
than to try and wear the halo.
maybe it was something that he ate,
or sniffed, or soaked up from tv
that makes his eyes flash *'it's late,*
it's feeding time'
in the restaurant of the dead community.
janie's friendly body
doesn't want to be alone,
she's a fountain of ideas
and all them gods designed her hormones,
but the neighbours just don't hold with queers
or strong ladies, gentle men
or other kinds of freak
who spoil largactyl lifetimes
by letting go their fears
and who break the seals
upon their lips to speak.
just because i'm paranoid

it doesn't cancel what i know
about political magicians
and their wands,
who stir rat poison up with h2o
to keep the crazies fighting
in the scum upon the pond.
this should be sci-fi, mister,
sister, but it's real:
the masters of the universe
have got us running on the wheel.

Molecular

it was like when the sea pulls back
and leaves the seabed grooved.
there was a pillow with a heartbeat
when i woke up and moved,
and physical clues everywhere.
the old me was officially missing, nowhere,
and like a bed of embers, you were there,
red lip-prints everywhere,
giving you away.
curtains behaved like the dress you wore
– they first hid, then revealed, the sun.
just like the dress you wore the night before
first hid and then revealed the sun.
i knew something heavy had been done
because the mattress was two-people warm,
and there were moans
in faint, new, alien tones,
and fingerprints and scratches.
in a forensic flash of light i blinked and smiled.
nothing much had been moved or changed,
except now there was beauty in the eye of the beholder.
walking straight off the set of a tv memory,
limited policemen began to try to chalk our shapes.
but we were molecular,
too strange and fluid.

Not for all the e's in england

not for all the e's in england,
not for all the cigarettes in france,
not for all the hollow ring of hollywood,
not for all the white folk who can't dance,
not for all the blowjobs in the whitehouse,
not for all the porn on the net,
not for all the sadists in religion,
would i erase the day we met.
not for all the guns in alabama,
not for all the stale sex in sales,
not for all the kids in catholic families,
not for all the sheep in wales,
not for all the drunken songs of exiles,
not for all the coppers on the take,
not for all the deep-fried food in glasgow,
would i say our love was a mistake.
not for all the sweat on vegas elvis,
not for all the chinese who drink tea,
not for all the rizla in jamaica,
not for all the fears that cripple me,
not for all the crap in capitalism,
not for all the stars that ever shone,
not for all the gangsters golden fillings,
would i suggest we carried on.

No picnic

we go for a walk in the park
and it's no walk in the park.
we take oysters and fine wines
into enchanted woods
but even that's no fucking picnic.
if music be the food of love, then honey,
someone's switched the tapes
and industrial noises serenade us
as we feast on sour grapes.
"you should get a job with the u.n.
you're so good at giving ultimata".
- "you should be a weatherman,
you're choc-full of bullshit data".
just when we think we've cleared the air
someone revs up a hidden tank
and a love-hate shell explodes and spits
a ton of sand where my heart just sank.
just when we think the sun is rising
a nuclear reactor cracks and leaks
and shadows mug us,
like slick ninja,
and *'i don't care'*
and you won't speak.
it doesn't matter how we mix
the mixture or how well we bake,
we could dust with this thing
with shit or sugar
- it'll never be a piece of cake.

Mister, you're a lapdancer

as i run down
your back
a clever tongue
i taste a sour patch of small print
which says *"this won't last long*
- you're too scared.
you mind the gap too much,
you never board the train,
you specialise
in hellos and goodbyes,
you're always wrapped up
against the rain.
i'm not flattered
by your attentive strokes
they're just technique and guile,
you're like a mobile hairdresser
- you want to make strangers smile
and feel beautiful.
mister, you're a lapdancer,
your moves are staged and dutiful.
you're a flight-only travel agent,
you can't even spell accommodation,
so wipe your spit
from off my back
and cancel my reservation".

The ghost of billy whizz

i've got memories of billy whizz
in his shit suit, selling his commodities.
a minor star in the chemical showbiz,
there's a new dealer where his ghost is.
he was six feet and eight stone,
just rocket fuel and skin and bone,
hardly one of heaven's own,
now his stupid name's in stone.
billy whizz is dead. long live the new dealer.
go crown yourself with nike and fila,
good luck, make money, mac, marina.
(he got harpooned by a hypo in the afternoon)
you can have too much of a good thing,
sweet teeth keep the death bell ringing,
but the clever boys learn how to swing
– so that means billy never did.
he was dedicated
to the pleasures of the citizens down town;
the dancers and the drifters,
urban sailors and the drowned.
and they raised a mental statue
to their psychoactive clown
and it dissolved in thunderbird
and methadone and brown.
he was half-caste, sure, half speed/half dope.
a line of white for waking up,
a smoke of black to cope
(with waking up).
it didn't wake you up this time,
and it killed more than your dick,
you were five days dead in summer
and you made your neighbours sick
– so nothing changes.
you were harpooned by a hypo

in the sunny afternoon.
if billy'd had a silver spade
he could've dug a groove and not his grave,
but wishing never helps – and nor does england.
it just files away the figures
on the fallen and the fucked,
like a monster in the ocean
with a taste for self-destruct.
he should've been another boy,
'smart sam' or *'clever roy'*,
but the tattoo artist he employed
was right – just *'billy whizz'*.
the very picture of an abstract painting,
still, he never set the ladies fainting,
except the ones who found him
feeding flies and writers much too soon,
harpooned by a hypo in the sunny afternoon.
roll the credits, let the headstone say
"armani and an office
could have brought it all his way.
he could have hit the big time, uk or usa
he should have worked for the cia"
– then the stray dog could have had its day –
he could have sold drugs to the whole world.
billy whizz is dead.
long live the new dealer.

Small times

Without trace

tracey, tracey, how she scared me.
I don't know why but she still can.
a bit too much like a broken record player,
her tongue can spit like so much bacon in the pan.
her learned behaviour is the kind that's taught
by teachers blindly chalking up the scars,
pouring petrol on a burning school of thought
and sending out the kids to play with cars.
we met when we were working in a chip van,
she scared the shit out of me at first
– so many knives, so little time to reason,
so everything i said was well-rehearsed.
i felt like little lord fauntleroy in velvet,
sweetsmelling, smart and royal with my talk,
kidnapped by a crazy, gin-soaked gargoyle
– i swear there was a boxer in her walk.
but doctor, she's in touch with her feelings,
when she's happy she roars out the latest hits,
charms bouncers with *"i hope you like the ceiling,*
chuck, 'cos i'm gonna ride you
'til you're drowning in me tits"
– and she's never seen a shrink yet.
happiness is a clean floor and a cashed-up till,
a lump of draw like half a loaf of bread,
a joke about a sausage and a laugh like asthma
and a call from the dibble to say that *'he's dead'.*
it's dead easy to patronise.
the noble savage has an easy face to draw,
you could file her under *'diamond, rough'*
just next to *'tart with heart'*
and other one-dee characters with a user-friendly flaw
– but she'd only twat you.
without trace

the world would be a nicer,
calmer, smoother, safer, better-spoken place.

Living in sin

a late night science programme
told me you were coming,
said that i should watch the skies
'something's going to break the earth a little',
spread perfume like a personal meteorite.
i'd been kind of living in a flat,
then you broke in and trashed all that.
without an iron swing-ball,
dynamite or crane,
you killed the horizontal lifestyle
and from the rubble you pulled fun
and sex and the risk of pain.
i thank you, madam,
for the way you did me in,
i may pay a little rent to the state angels,
but you let me live for free in sin.
seems like you stole
and sold my old flat life,
and stashed hot mountains
in my council property.
jesus! himalayas in my bedroom,
rivers running down our sides.
a better kind of opium for my masses,
from concrete
you raised high savannah grasses.
just like the san andreas fault
and pulp romance, you moved the earth,
put contour lines on my life's map,
you splashed me
with the smell of hell and pleasure
and then you pulled me
through a you-shaped gap.
supermodels? supermodels? supermodels
and the oxygen in heaven are too thin –

they kill juicy beauty and always have an alibi.
so i'll be laughing in the living room of sin
with the one whose make-up makes the saints cry.

Ingland strip

i've been watching a film
called 'tombstone, ingland'
and in the first scene the hero dies.
i'm in a sawn-off highrise,
using my closed-circuit eyes.
the son sinks 'night nurse' in the west,
dogs on valium make last requests,
terry's medals scratch his chest
and who remembers the war?
– well, he does.
he got the pox in county antrim,
he got burned on tumbledown,
he lost a leg in a desert storm
now he's waiting for the crown
– the crowning glory –
you know the story.
ironic, home, on the fourteenth floor
that he should now start suffering more.
home, just near vera,
and vera dies in the deep white cold
and someone says it's because she's old,
but if her rings had been real gold
she could've had a flat
that wasn't just a fridge and a museum.
real gold, treasure in the people's soul
and someone's nicked because they stole
some bread and beans to fill a hole
and it wasn't even organic.
at sixty-seven, ted's ashamed,
the local paper, for a change,
spelt someone's name correctly.
old thief, he tries to weep away the grief
and wipes the clock that he received
for forty years of being deceived

in *'faithful service'*.
it all goes down the garbage chute together.
meanwhile, down there somewhere,
young lovers tongue in a tight embrace.
glue and kisses scent his face.
she smiles, pulls tight on her puppy's lead
and takes the strain as he shoots his seed
– she'll always take the strain.
the knackered lift was the nuptial suite
and she conceives at a hundred feet
"honeymoon, honey, on the thirteenth floor?"
it's all the rage with the urban poor.
in tombstone, ingland, ingland's born
while vacant tv hosts
ask *'just how hard is porn?'*
the vertical village is left to mourn
the birth of the child of gaz 'n' dawn.
the baby's only just alive
but he's got his name down for a '45.
relief queues snake forever longer,
tagged and shagged
but doin' the conga
along the hard shoulder from bed to bookies,
veterans showing ropes to rookies.
a few lines left and the story limps
– it's been arguing with someone's pimp.
it falls near mary who is wearing cider
and this raconteur reclines beside her.
in *'tombstone, ingland'* ingland lives,
but including me and you
who gives?

Kenny and the snake

you'll never offer kenny anything twice
– he doesn't mind if he does.
like a magician he will open your eyes
to unimagined phenomena
like the *"spare pint"* and *"a room you don't need"*.
in the lost city from where, one day, he hitched south,
with a sign saying *'north'*, everyone is like kenny.
the economy is based on an intricate and ancient system,
the principle manifestation of which
is the repeated act of borrowing.
it is considered macabre and virtually taboo
to make overt attempts to repay
and lending is seen in a similar light to indecent exposure.
the rhythms of that society are too subtle
for precise explanation
but to observe the population in action
is very much like watching oriental opera
– there are many slow, reluctant movements
and frequent looks of astonishment.
the army of kenny's lost city is armed with cheap guitars
and two tunes.
at times of crisis fifty thousand highly irregular soldiers
share a borrowed PA and tune up on the frontier for weeks
"wun-two, wun-two, two, two"
crackling through the valleys like bursts of lead.
there has never been a successful invasion.
looking on the bright side you will be exposed
to a dynamic range of emotions
when kenny comes for *'a few days'* and two weeks later
he will have helped you become a better person
and you'll have an altogether higher opinion of yourself.
the snake that he keeps in a plastic bag
will have escaped a couple of times
and you will have started to be amused

by the fact that he was given it in part-payment
for a decorating job.
it is not venomous but you will have wondered
if the snake-donor knew this.
you will never offer kenny anything twice
- he doesn't mind if he does.
asking him to leave, conversely, requires regular repetition
over the space of a lunar month,
and eventually when he goes
you'll feel like you've given birth.
you will walk around the flat, exhaling deeply,
saying things like: *"fu-cking hell"*
and checking you still have certain things.
whilst reclaiming your territory you will find
an un-stamped postcard
stuffed down the side of the chair he slept in,
addressed to the eventual inheritors of his estate.
it will say that daddy is staying with a very nice friend
who is helping him a lot.
You will be kicked in the nuts by guilt and feel cheap,
but you will get over it.
a week later you will see a young man
in a dayglo orange anorak lying face up
in the style of the crucified
between a shoe shop and the billboard
for a significant hollywood release.
you will ask him what the crack is
and he will roll over to reveal a chalk blur
which he is trying to protect from the pouring rain.
"doin' a bit of art, bud, tryin' to get a few quid.
gotta get some rats for the snake".
slightly like lovers, your eyes will meet
and the word 'smack'
will be spoken, silently,
with a hiss.

Ritual abuse

i've been ritually abused,
i signed on like it was a career.
i had a very fluid signing action,
my advisor called me *'claimant of the year'*.
and she was always yawning.
i'd say *"yeah, baby, i'd rather be in bed as well*
- but not with you,
just give me the pen and i'll make my mark
and slow-waltz the fortnight through".
now i don't mind not working.
i can take crap jobs or leave them.
it's just the circus hoops
you have to leap through,
the strokes you have to pull,
and the fact that monkeys eat the peanuts
before you receive them.
but i do mind the old *'new deal'* –
take a shit job or tread the breadline,
give head or forget the meal
– that stinks, i think,
but that's politics.
i've been ritually abused,
i had a christian education.
i was bored stiff by the priest's *'good news'*
and tasted brimstone after masturbation.
meanwhile the preacher got his kicks
and terrestrially paid
for serving up the s'n'm, the bondage,
and mentally screwing
the congregation while it prayed.
now i can almost handle some ideas of god,
i might have one myself called *'brave love'*.
but i don't dig the way we sow the heads of kids
with a seed called *'christ'*,

and get them early,
get them used to having a big strong man above.
but that's religion
(and politics).
i've been ritually abused,
i have read the daily papers,
and i've breathed in the family drugs
while the fiction barons raped us.
they've said to me *"we love you, darling briton,*
you're a chip off the western bloc",
and it's the same hand that pats you on the head
that leads you by the cock.
and over breakfast i've seen the breasts
of a girl just turned sixteen,
falling out into my cornflakes
while the headlines boldly scream
"cage the sex fiends!", *"smash the strikers!"*,
"for perverts - the noose!",
and best of all, *"we lift the lid on ritual abuse"*.
but that's newspapers
(and religion)
(and politics).

Slaves made my baby's shoes

so damn the kids in country x,
let's blur the line between work and sex.
they say that omelettes don't get made
unless some chicken, or its egg, gets laid
and broken.
some things,
no matter how routinely they are left unspoken,
sound like 'slave'.
but the sweet figure of net gains
for third parties who take pains
soothes the awkward rattle of the chains
for the spectators.
i've got some good/bad, good/bad, good/bad news:
i've got a baby and slaves make her shoes.
i blame the blacks, the whites
the chinese, the arabs and the jews:
i've got a baby and slaves made her shoes.
screw the little lady in her cage,
let's widen roads and deepen rage.
the web's for porn and family trees
and seeing strangers arse-up on their knees, and working.
it's necrophilia, the bird is on the wire
but this shit isn't 'lucky', it's just shit.
and I blame the spooks, the spics, the WASPS,
the weather and the age,
and I have a little look
and the bird is on the wire,
the girl is in the cage.
I've got some good/bad, good/bad, good/bad news:
I've got a baby and slaves make her shoes.

Spectacular times

we're the punters that watch the crimes,
domestic boxing, broken love and working pantomimes.
eyes wide when the camera shines
in these spectacular times.
the hard baby with the bombs and the tv
sold me a state of emergency,
there's a dollar beating where a heart should be
and i don't know why i'm here, popped up on fear.
i'm hanging over the box of delights,
hung over, like a vulture,
as if the cathode ray could shed some light
or plug me into a touching culture.
i'm slipping in the places in the spaces in between
the cash crop job-psychosis
and the deep blue marine
and the welfare cheque's the pulse
upon the life-support machine
while the hard baby wails like satan
round a land that ain't so green.
us lovers sometimes use our loves as 3D alibis
or excuses for the silence or the violence or the lies.
my leader loves me, so he's putting bombers in the skies
and i'm laughing at the versions of us, locked in our eyes.
i don't make so many plans because each day is just a fuse
and sexy missiles in the silos are just dying to be used
and not much ever happens how you want it to,
not much ever happens how you always thought it might do.
we've got machine guns but we need musicians
to sing us some songs about sex and sedition,
a molotov ballad and a whole new tradition
and a tune to defeat the hard baby.
maybe it's just gravity that keeps me down
or maybe it's the aristos and their thorny crown
or maybe it's because

i've got to build my own jail town
in these progressive times,
in these spectacular times.

Little rockets

i work a factory, she works the streets
and we are held apart
by two labels for the same meat.
we only meet in our unspoken symmetry,
unacquainted stars,
we share the same trajectory,
little rockets, stabbing at the mystery,
you couldn't fit a dollar bill between us.
(oh but if you'd seen us
like we sometimes see ourselves)
mister takes a dictionary,
reads out *'sucker'* – does he mean us?
he's a master of the x-ray
and he loves the way he's seen us.
clocking on or going down
like a dime-a-dozen venus,
pleasing the man
in ways that he should not be pleased,
then by his god we are teased.
hooker and machine man
pick up pennies for their pains
and leave the pieces of the people
they could be to dream of spain,
and spin the wheel of fortune
down the big old loser's lane,
and crash into the barriers of cash.
steel bodies we don't have
but we protect our little ships.
i think of strikes and sabotage
and she says *"not on the lips"*.
because even while you're being screwed
you can build a barricade
with the bits you don't include.